POWERPACK

Puppet power

Twenty-four puppet sketches

Kevin Mayhew

POWERPACK

With special thanks to Jim and Mary Aldwinckle, Peter, Chris and Nick Jackson, who have written this collection of puppet sketches. They have been used with great success in Powerpack meetings, family services, school assemblies, etc., and have proved to be a valuable resource for any children's ministry.

First published in 2000 by
KEVIN MAYHEW LTD
Buxhall
Stowmarket
Suffolk IP14 3BW

0 1 2 3 4 5 6 7 8 9

ISBN 1 84003 629 X
Catalogue No 1500386

Cover design by Jonathan Stroulger
Edited and typeset by Elisabeth Bates
Printed and bound in Great Britain

CONTENTS

INTRODUCTION

The value of puppets

Puppets have enormous value for effective communication. Used within the context of a balanced programme they appeal to all ages. They can be used to initiate or to reinforce a point, portraying real life situations. Children readily identify with the puppets and may well talk to a puppet when they would not talk to an adult, thereby also making them a useful tool in difficult counselling situations.

A child's concentration span is said to be approximately one minute per year of their age (that is at an optimum level), but experience has shown that this can be extended by the use of puppets mainly because they are such a visual means of communication.

Another advantage of using puppets is that just a minimum of props are required, while the only major disadvantage is the limited number of movements possible.

The use of puppets

A puppet theatre is traditionally associated with 'puppet shows' but is not a necessity and in fact can limit movement. Puppets can be used in a variety of ways, either on their own or with drama. They can speak in one of three ways:

1. The puppet pretends to talk to the operator (whispers in his/her ear), i.e. the operator interacts with the puppet.
2. The operator interacts with the puppet and is the voice of the puppet.
3. The operator can be just the manipulator and voice of the puppet and puppets can interact with one another.

Practical Tips

- Hold the puppet quite high so that it can easily be seen.
- Be careful not to block the audience's view of the puppet. Stand behind it rather than at the side.
- Don't worry if your lips move – there's no need to be a ventriloquist! The children will be far more interested in the puppet than in you!

- Practise in front of a mirror before using a puppet. Remember to move the puppet's mouth as you speak!
- Practise portraying different emotional states with your puppet, e.g. shyness, happiness, fear, anger . . .
- Decide on a name and character for your puppet and keep to it. A change in name or character can cause confusion and an inability to identify.
- Be careful to talk puppet to puppet rather than operator to operator.
- Always learn the script if you can.
- Choose puppets that are appropriate to the size of your group, e.g. small hand puppets are ideal for a small group of children but unsuitable for a family church service or large meeting because of visibility.
- You can even use ordinary soft toys without a glove or an open mouth – especially with very young children.

The scripts contained in this book are some which we have written and used successfully in Powerpack meetings. Much of the time we 'ad lib' sketches and therefore scripting these for others to use has proved difficult in some cases. However, you are at liberty to alter or adapt these sketches to suit your own situation, personnel, etc. You will also need to update or change some of the names or objects mentioned, making them relevant to your own particular group, e.g. Manchester United is mentioned in one or two sketches and could be changed to your local football club. Also Beanie Babies are the subject of 'The Garage Sale' and, although popular at the moment, that may need to be changed in time to something more current. You will also need to change the names of the puppets to those of your own.

ALL CHANGE

Teaching points

- changing your mind
- disloyalty
- unfaithfulness

Characters

Ernie (in blue football supporter's gear), Billy Joe and Mum

Enter Ernie chanting and cheering, football style.

E *(Sings)* City! . . . City! . . . City! . . . *(Shouts)* Come on you Blues! . . . etc.

BJ Whatever are you doing?

E *(Singing)* We won, we won, we won, we won! . . . etc.

BJ You can't shout for City!

E Why not?

BJ Because you support United!

E Not any more.

BJ What?

E Brilliant game. You should have seen those five goals – fantastic! Top of the league we'll be now.

BJ Traitor! Just because they're going to win the league. Hey! Wait a minute! What about the tickets you asked me to get, for us to go and see United's cup match?

E Don't want them.

BJ But they cost me ten pounds each.

E That's your loss. I'm not going. Who'd want to see *them* anyway?

BJ *You* did . . . yesterday!

E Yes, but I've changed my mind, haven't I?

BJ You could at least give me the money for one of the tickets.

E No way! Get someone else to go with you. Anyway, I said I'd go and see Barney.

BJ *(Sarcastically)* Unless you change your mind!

Enter Mum

M What are you two squabbling about?

BJ It's him. He's changed sides and won't give me the money for the football ticket I bought him. And it cost ten pounds!

E Wouldn't go if you paid me. *(Sings)* City! . . . City! . . . City! . . . etc.

M Ernie, stop it! You can't just change your mind like that.

E Why not?

M Because it's not fair. Billy Joe's relying on you to go with him.

E Too bad. I'm not going. Wouldn't want to watch United now anyway.

M Well that's a pity, because I thought I would treat you and Billy Joe to a meal out at McDonald's after the match.

E McDonald's?

M But if you're not going, then . . .

E A whole meal at McDonalds?

M Yes.

E With chocolate milkshake?

M Yes.

E *(Tearing off blue scarf, etc.)* Come on you Reds! United! . . . United! . . . United!

M *(Amazed)* But you were supporting City a minute ago!

E Well . . . I've changed my mind!!

Exit Mum, Billy Joe and Ernie.

BELIEVE IT OR NOT!

Teaching points
- unbelief
- believing is seeing!

Characters
Billy Joe and Ernie

Props
2 paper bags

Enter Billy Joe and Ernie with paper bags on their heads.

BJ Nice day.

E Yes.

BJ Sun's hot.

E What?

BJ Sun's hot, isn't it?

E What sun? What do you mean?

BJ You know, the sun in the sky.

E The sun in the sky? What's a sun?

BJ Not *a* sun – *the* sun. There's only one sun, isn't there?

E I don't know – I don't know what you're talking about.

BJ That big yellow ball in the sky. That's what I'm talking about.

E Big yellow ball? How big?

BJ 1,400,000km across, actually.

E You're joking. That's bigger than the earth!

BJ Yep. 100 times bigger!

E Wow! And it's in the sky, you say?

BJ Yes.

E I don't believe you.

BJ It's true.

E How do you know?

BJ I heard about it.

E Oh, you'll believe anything, you will.

BJ It's true I tell you.

E Well I can't see it.

BJ You don't have to see it to know it's there.

E What does it do then, this sun?

BJ It keeps us warm.

E My jumper keeps me warm.

BJ It gives us light as well, you know, so we can see where we're going.

E Well I can't see it. I'll believe it when I see it!

BJ Well, let's take our bags off then.

E I'm quite happy with mine *on*, actually.

BJ Oh, come on. I've heard a lot about the sun, I'd like to see it.

E Oh all right, I'll try anything once, but I'm not convinced.

Billy Joe and Ernie take the bags off their heads only to find that it's dark.

E Well, where is this sun then? It's pitch black!

BJ Oh, this must be night-time.

E Night-time?

BJ Yes. That's when the sun goes round the other side for a few hours.

E The other side of what?

BJ The earth.

E But we're standing on the earth.

BJ Yes, I know.

E So if it's round the other side, you mean it's underneath us at this very moment?

BJ Well sort of.

E You are crazy. Honestly, the stuff you believe is just . . . unbelievable!

BJ Oh come on. Look, it'll be back in a few hours and we can see it. Really!

E You must be joking. I'm going back the way I was.

Ernie puts his bag back on his head.

BJ Oh don't do that. Look . . . it's getting brighter now. It'll be out soon.

E Don't talk rubbish. I've heard enough of your fairy stories.

BJ Oh don't be like that. Can't you feel it getting warmer?

E No, not really.

BJ Oh look, it's coming! Take your bag off, Ernie, it's lovely.

E Not likely.

BJ Wow! It's just as good as everyone said it was. Come on, Ernie, you're missing a treat.

E Oh, I'm going.

Exit Ernie still with his bag on his head.

BJ Well . . . just look what he's missing! Believing is seeing after all!

Exit Billy Joe.

DO AS YOU'RE TOLD!

Teaching points
- obedience
- dangers of watching some TV programmes
- Mother's Day

Characters
Ernie and Florrie

Props
remote control, television

Ernie and Florrie sit watching television, facing the audience.

E Eh! I love this programme!

F Mum said we weren't to watch this after last week.

E Oh go on – she'll never know. She's out in the kitchen. Turn the sound down.

F Have you forgotten what happened last week?

E What?

F After you'd watched all that fighting, you and Gilbert had a big fight. And you got hurt, remember?

E Oh that! That was nothing.

F You didn't think that at the time.

E We . . . ll! Ssh! I can't hear!

F But I don't want to watch this.

E Tough!

F Anyway, you promised Mum that you wouldn't watch! Eh, and what about that Mother's Day card you sent.

E What about it?

F All that stuff you wrote about *(sarcastically)* – how much you loved her and that you'd do anything for her!

E Well?

F Well, perhaps you should do as she says then!

E Oh, stop making me feel guilty.

F Anyway, I'm not watching it! Let's see what's on the other side. *(Grabs remote control and changes channels)*

E *(Annoyed)* Oi!

Pause to watch. Then both puppets begin to laugh.

E Oh great! I love this programme!

F Yeah! So do I! *(Both puppets laugh)*

Exit Ernie and Florrie.

DON'T BE AFRAID

Teaching points

- God does not want us to be afraid
- resisting God's enemy
- the power of God's word.

Characters
Ernie, Mum and Snake.

Ernie playing in his bedroom. Enter Mum.

M Come on now, Ernie, it's bedtime.

E Oh, but Mum . . . can I have five more minutes?

M You've had five more minutes. Now into bed or you'll never be able to get up for school in the morning.

E *(Groans)* Oh all right. *(Lays down)*

M Goodnight, Ernie.

E Goodnight, Mum.

Exit Mum. Ernie falls asleep and starts to snore. Enter Snake stealthily, creeping up behind Ernie.

S *(In an evil-sounding voice)* Hey, kid!

E *(Wakes with a start)* What? Who's that?

S There's a sssnake under your bed.

Exit Snake.

E What? A snake? Where? *(Looks under bed)* Yes, there is! It's a s . . . s . . . snake! Mum! . . . Mum! . . . MUM! *(Frantic shouts)*

Enter Mum.

M What's the matter, Ernie?

E There . . . there . . . there's a s . . . s . . . s . . . snake u . . . under my b . . . b . . . bed!

M There's a snake under your bed? Oh really, Ernie. Let me have a look. *(Picks up imaginary sock)* Oh, Ernie, it's only your dirty sock! Pooh!

E *(Relieved)* Oh! Thank goodness for that.

M Now lie down and go straight back to sleep. Night-night.

Exit Mum. Ernie settles down to sleep again, muttering 'just a silly sock'. Soon begins snoring again. Enter Snake.

S Hey, kid!

E *(Startled)* Eh? What? Who's that?

S There's a burglar at the window.

Exit Snake.

E *(In a panic)* A . . . a . . . a . . . burglar? At the w . . . w . . . window? *(Freezes)* Oh yes, I can hear a t . . . t . . . tapping noise. Mum! . . . Mum! . . . MUM!

Enter Mum

M Dear me, Ernie, whatever's the matter now?

E There . . . there . . . there's a b . . . b . . . b . . . burglar at the w . . . w . . . window.

M Oh Ernie, don't be silly.

E There . . . there is. I . . . I . . . I can hear a t . . . t . . . tapping noise. Li . . . li . . . listen!

M *(Listening)* Let's open the curtains, shall we? *(Opens imaginary curtains)* There you are, Ernie – no burglar – just a twig tapping against the window. It's just a bit windy tonight.

E *(Relieved)* Oh! Oh yes. Thank you, Mum.

M Now no more worries, Ernie. Lie down. Night-night.

Exit Mum. Ernie goes off to sleep again, muttering 'just a silly old twig'. Soon he begins to snore. Enter Snake.

S Hey, kid!

E *(Startled)* Who? What? Who's there?

S There's a monster in your wardrobe.

Exit Snake.

E (In a panic) A . . . a . . . m . . . m . monster? I . . . i . . . in the w . . . w . . . wardrobe? *(Looks towards imaginary wardrobe and freezes)* Oh no! Look! I can s . . . s . . . see him. Mum! . . . Mum! . . . MUM!

Enter Mum.

M Ernie! Whatever's wrong with you tonight?

E There . . . there . . . there's a m . . . monster in the w . . . w . . . wardrobe! Look!

M Oh Ernie, that's your dressing-gown hanging up.

E *(Relieved)* Oh! Oh, so it is. Thank you, Mum.

M I don't know what's wrong with you tonight, Ernie, but you are so frightened. Do you remember that verse from the Bible that you learned in Powerpack *(Sunday school/club, etc.)* last week?

E Er . . .

M You know, the one about not being afraid.

Mum helps Ernie repeat the verse.

E Oh yes. *(Hesitatingly)* 'Do not be . . . afraid . . . I am with you . . . I am your God.' . . . Um! . . . 'Do not be terrified for the Lord your God is with you wherever you go.'

M That's it. Well, every time you feel afraid, speak it out. You'll soon feel better.

E OK. Thanks, Mum. Night-night.

M Goodnight, Ernie.

Exit Mum. Ernie settles down to sleep as before. Enter Snake.

S Hey, kid!

E *(Startled)* What?

S There's a snake under your bed.

Ernie starts to panic but then remembers to say the Bible verse, if a little nervously. Snake, obviously a little shaken, backs away. Ernie begins to settle down again. Snake tries again.

S Hey, kid! There's a burglar at the window.

Ernie speaks out the verse a little more confidently. Snake recoils.

E Mmm! It works. *(Settles down)*

Snake tries again.

S Hey, kid! There's a monster in the wardrobe.

E *(Ernie shouts at the snake)* 'Do not be afraid, I am with you. I am your God. Do not be terrified for the Lord your God is with you wherever you go!'

Snake runs off with a scream. Exit Ernie.

EMELINE'S BIRTHDAY

Teaching points
- loving God and giving him the best
- thoughtfulness/thoughtlessness!

Characters
Ernie, Gilbert, Jasper, Billy Joe and Adult

Props
old penknife, bone, perfume in carrier bag
2 neatly wrapped presents

Enter Adult with a wrapped present, talking ad lib to audience about it being Emeline's birthday. Enter Jasper carrying a bone.

A Oh, Jasper, I hope you've remembered it's Emeline's birthday today!

J 'Course I have! *(Holds out the bone)* Look! I've bought her this!

A You can't give Emeline a bone, Jasper!

J Why not? I'd love a bone if it was my birthday.

A But she's a little girl?

J I know that!

A Little girls don't eat bones!

J Don't they? Why not?

A Oh Jasper. Only dogs eat bones!

J Oh, right! I'd better go and eat it then!

Exit Jasper, muttering that Emeline doesn't know what she's missing!

A Well! Whatever next! Here comes Ernie. I hope he's remembered.

Enter Ernie with penknife in his pocket.

A Hi, Ernie. Have you remembered that it's Emeline's birthday today?

E Oh no! I've forgotten!

A Oh, Ernie, you haven't! I reminded you yesterday.

E Oh, what shall I do? I know! *(Takes out penknife from his pocket)* I've just found this at the park. I'll give her this!

A Ernie, you can't give her an old rusty penknife. It's dangerous, and anyway I'm sure Emeline wouldn't really want a penknife!

E Yeah, I think she will. She loved that carving my dad did. And now she'll be able to do one herself.

A But Ernie, she's too young to use a penknife.

E I'll just go and wrap it up.

Exit Ernie, not listening.

A Oh dear, this isn't very good so far.

Enter Gilbert with a cheap-looking carrier bag.

A Hi, Gilbert! Have you remembered that it's Emeline's birthday today?

G Sure have. I've got her present in this bag. I'm just off to give it to her.

A Oh, but Gilbert, that bag doesn't look very special.

G I know. But I didn't have any money left to buy pretty wrapping paper.

A Oh, I see. You must have got her something very special then. What is it?

G *(Whispers)* It's perfume.

A Oh, very nice, Gilbert. She'll love that.

G Yes. I took one of Mum's half-empty bottles and topped it up with water. *(Looks around secretively and takes out perfume)* Look!

A Gilbert! Really! Whatever will you think of next? That's not very good, giving her watered-down perfume.

G Oh, she'll never know!

A I think she will.

G Well, that's all I've got. I had to buy a new football this week so I'd got no money. Anyway, I'd better go and find her 'cos I'm off down the park in a minute to play with my new football.

Exit Gilbert, calling 'Emeline – happy birthday!'

A Well! This gets worse! Jasper has got something for Emeline that *he* would like; Ernie forgot and is giving her a penknife, of all things! And now Gilbert is giving her watered-down perfume . . .

Enter Billy Joe with a beautifully wrapped present.

BJ Hey, Chris *(Use appropriate Adult's name)*, guess what I've bought for Emeline's birthday?

A What?

BJ A Barbie doll settee. *(Substitute other suitable present)*

A Oh, Billy Joe, that's just what she wants. She'll love it.

BJ Yes. I've been thinking for a long time about what she'd really like because she always buys us such nice things.

A I'm so glad you've remembered, Billy Joe. At least she'll have *some* nice presents.

Exit Adult and Billy Joe.

ERNIE'S BAD TEMPER

Teaching points

- need for self-control
- a gentle answer will calm a person's anger

Characters

Mum, Ernie, Snake and Florrie

Enter Mum and Ernie.

M Ernie, I thought I told you to put your bike away.

E I did, Mum.

M Well, how comes I've just fallen over it in the garden.

E I don't know. I did put it away in the shed, honestly.

M But you couldn't have done or I wouldn't have fallen over it, would I? Look, I've got a big bruise on my leg now.

E Florrie must have got it out then.

M Now don't go blaming your sister.

E Well, she's always taking my things and getting me into trouble. It's not fair!

M Why should she want your bike anyway? She's got a nice bike of her own.

E I know. Her bike is better than mine! Why does Florrie always get the best things?

M Stop grumbling, Ernie, and next time do as you're told straight away.

Exit Mum. Enter Snake.

S *(To audience)* I'm going to see if I can make Ernie really angry. *(To Ernie)* That wasn't fair was it?

E No, it wasn't!

S I bet you're feeling angry now, aren't you?

E Yes, I am. Florrie's always getting me into trouble. She never gets into trouble 'cos she's the favourite.

S Yes, and she's got a better bike than yours.

E I know. It makes me really angry.

S Good. That's right, you get angry.

E I am. I'm really mad now! You just wait 'til I see Florrie. I'll give her what for.

S Yes, go on. That's the way! Have a good shout at her. Look, here she comes now. I'm off!

Exit Snake.

E Right, Florrie – I'm hopping mad now. You just wait!

Enter Florrie.

F Hiya.

E *(Angrily)* What do you think you're doing, getting my bike out and pretending you never did, and getting me into trouble? You rotten little sister, you. I hate you.

F I never did.

E Oh yes you did – because I put it in the shed like I was told to and then Mum fell over it and bruised her leg. So who did it, eh? Eh? Are you trying to tell me the budgie got it out!

F No, I got it out.

E You just said you never did!

F No. I meant I never pretended not to do it.

E Well, you just go and tell Mum it was you, then, 'cos she thinks it was me. And I'm really angry now. You're always getting me into trouble – and anyway it's not fair – your bike is much better than mine.

F Mum doesn't think it was you. I just told her it was me – she's just asked.

E Do you mean she's not blaming me after all?

F No, she's not. She knows it was me. Do you really think my bike is better than yours?

E Yes, I do and it's not fair!

F Well, do you want to swap bikes? Because I like your bike better than mine.

E Do you really?

F Yes. Shall we swap?

E Yeah!

F OK. You're not still angry with me, are you?

E No – I'm sorry. I get into a really bad temper sometimes.

F I know, and it's horrible to live with.

E Sorry! Friends?

F Friends! Come on, let's swap our bikes now.

Exit Ernie and Florrie.

FLORRIE AND THE BLACKMAIL!

Teaching point
• always be honest and tell the truth

Characters
Mum, Florrie, Gilbert and Billy Joe

Props
jewellery box, ring (to fit puppet's finger!)
50p (optional)

Mum and Florrie, looking at Grandma's jewellery.

F Cor, Mum, Grandma's old jewellery must be worth a fortune!

M Well, not really *that* much. But it's worth a lot to me because it's all I've got left of my mum's things.

F Coo, it's lovely! Look at this lovely ring.

M Look, I must go and get on – I've still got your sandwiches to make for school. Put the jewellery away when you've finished looking at it.

F Mum, can I wear this ring to school today?

M No, certainly not! You know you mustn't wear jewellery for school anyway, let alone precious family heirlooms.

Exit Mum, stage right.

F Oh this ring is lovely. *(Puts ring on finger)* I'm going to take it to school anyway and show it to my best friend. She'll love it. Mum will never know.

Exit Florrie, stage left.

Later that day.

Re-enter Florrie, looking for the ring. Enter Gilbert, stage right.

F Oh no! Where's Grandma's ring? Oh no, I can't have lost it. Oh dear, whatever can I do? My mum'll go spare when she knows; she'll kill me! I'll be grounded for a year . . . Oh dear! *(Starts to cry)*

G What's up with you?

F Oh, Gilbert, you must help me. I brought my Grandma's old ring to school to show my friend, and now I've lost it and my mum'll go bananas when she knows.

G Oh dear! What's it worth not to tell her?

F Gilbert, you can't tell my mum what I've done. You just can't!

G Well, give me 50p then and I won't tell.

F 50p?

G Yes, 50p or else I'm round your house straight after school telling your mum.

F Oh, you are so mean, Gilbert. Here you are – 50p – but don't you dare tell my mum about the ring.

G OK. See you tomorrow.

Exit Gilbert, stage right, and Florrie, stage left.

The next day.

Enter Gilbert and Florrie.

G Well, Florrie, have you got my 50p today?

F What do you mean?

G 50p not to tell your mum about the ring.

F But I gave you 50p yesterday.

G That was yesterday's 50p. I meant I wanted 50p *every* day.

F But I haven't got 50p today.

G Too bad, Florrie. I'll see you around your house tonight then. *(He leaves)*

F Now what am I going to do? *(Starts to cry)*

Enter Billy Joe.

BJ What's up, Florrie?

F Oh, it's that mean Gilbert. I brought this ring to school and I shouldn't have done, and now Gilbert's charging me 50p a day not to tell my mum what's happened. I just don't know what to do, Billy Joe.

BJ Well I think that you should tell your mum the truth.

F What?

BJ You must tell your mum exactly what's happened.

F But, Billy Joe, I can't! She'll kill me!

BJ No, she won't, Florrie. You must pray and ask the Holy Spirit to help you be strong, Florrie. Being honest and truthful is the only way to fight against evil – and Gilbert's really bad to blackmail you like that.

F Will you help me pray, Billy Joe; only I don't really know how to?

BJ Of course. 'Lord, please will you give Florrie the power to be strong and brave and to own up to what she has done wrong. Amen.'

F Thank you, Billy Joe. I suppose I'd better go and tell her now.

Exit Billy Joe, stage right, and Florrie, stage left.

At home.

Enter Mum and Florrie.

M Hi, Florrie. Have you had a good day at school?

F Not really, Mum. There's something I've got to tell you.

M I'm listening.

F You know Grandma's ring, and you said I mustn't take it to school?

M Yes.

F Well, I didn't take it off like you said because I wanted to take it and show it to Emeline. Only when I got to school I couldn't find it. And then Gilbert found out and he's blackmailing me. He said he would tell you if I didn't give him 50p. But then he wanted 50p every day!

M Oh dear! Well, I can put you out of your misery, Florrie. After you left for school, I found Grandma's ring on the floor, and so it's been in the jewellery box all the time. It isn't lost at all.

F It's not lost?

M No! So you can tell Gilbert that I know all about it anyway, and he's got nothing to blackmail you with. If you are honest and truthful, Florrie, no one can hold any threats over you.

F No, I see that now. I'm sorry, Mum, for disobeying. Thank you, Lord, for giving me strength to own up.

Exit Mum and Florrie.

FORGIVE AND FORGET

Teaching points

- importance of forgiveness
- not bearing grudges

Characters

Florrie and Emeline

Enter Florrie and Emeline, talking excitedly about Florrie's party.

F Mum says I've got to let her know who's coming to the party by tonight. So who shall I ask?

E Well there's Charlie and Jasper.

F Yes. And Sam and Penny.

E Ernie and Billy Joe.

F Yes.

E Oh and there's Eric.

F *(Hesitates)* Er . . . OK.

E And what about Gilbert?

F Gilbert? No way!

E Why?

F Well, look what happened last year.

E What?

F You must remember. He spoilt the whole party.

E Did he?

F	'Course he did. He messed about the whole of the time and cheated in all the games.
E	Oh yes, so he did – but that was last year.
F	And he broke my new Barbie doll. Don't you remember?
E	Yes . . . but he did say 'sorry'.
F	Well, it was a bit late after he'd broken it!
E	It was an accident.
F	Yes I know, but it was his fault. He was being silly and showing off.
E	Haven't you forgiven him for that yet?
F	No, why should I? And another thing – remember that time when we wanted him to come swimming and he made excuses?
E	Well?
F	Well, he didn't come, did he?
E	No – but he couldn't – his mum and dad were taking him out.
F	Huh! Some excuse! He just pleases himself. If he doesn't want to do something, he just makes excuses.
E	That's not fair!
F	And another thing. He didn't invite me to his party.
E	He didn't have one.
F	Well he wouldn't have done if he had!
E	'Course he would.

F No he wouldn't. And another thing – he took Sam out of our gang and stopped him being our friend.

E No he didn't – that was Sam's fault. Anyway, Gilbert was great fun when he came to my party.

F Well, I'm not inviting him to mine!

E He has changed, you know. He's OK. He'll be ever so disappointed. Go on – invite him.

F *(Reluctantly)* Oh, all right – but if he spoils things again that's him off my list for ever.

E He won't – you'll see.

Exit Florrie and Emeline, still talking about who to invite.

GILBERT'S NEW HEART

Teaching points
- the need to love one another
- being kind
- the importance of saying 'sorry'

Characters
Gilbert, Florrie, Emeline and Heart (or Conscience)

Enter Gilbert and Florrie.

G Watcha, Florrie!

F Hiya, Gilbert. What shall we do this playtime?

G Look, there's a new kid over there. Let's go and duff him up and see if he's got any dinner money.

F Gilbert! I'm surprised at you.

G Come on.

F No, I won't! He's only little and anyway it's wrong.

G I know he's only little, that's why it'll be easy. Come on.

F No!

G Chicken!

F No, I'm not chicken. It's a mean thing to do.

G *(Teasing)* Chicken!

F No, I'm not!

G You are!

F *(Indignantly)* No, I am not!

G *(Mocking)* Cowardy, cowardy custard!

F Stop it, Gilbert. What's got into you?

G *(Singing)* Who's a cowardy custard? Cowardy, cowardy custard!

F *(Becoming more upset)* Stop it!

G Goggle-eyes, big-nosed freak!

F Don't be so nasty!

G Smelly! Jelly-bellied jerk!

F *(More upset)* Oh! You're horrible!

G Cry baby! Cry baby! . . .

F You . . . you big ape! I thought you were supposed to be my friend! With friends like you, who needs enemies?

G Well clear off then! But before you do, I'll have your dinner money and your sweets. *(Snatches them away)*

F *(Cries)* Ohh! . . . *(Runs off)*

Pause while Gilbert congratulates himself and crams all the sweets into his mouth. Enter Emeline, looking very serious.

E *(American accent optional)* Hiya, Gilbert.

G Watcha, Emeline. You look miserable.

E I am. Well I am just so distressed and perplexed. Why I declare I don't know what to do!

G Why? What's up?

E Well, I have just met my friend. She was so upset! It seems that there's this real bad guy giving her a hard time.

G Well, there are some nasty folk around you know!

E You're telling me, Gilbert. Why, do you know, this guy even took my friend's dinner money and she's had no dinner today! She's starvin' hungry because of that mean guy!

G Well, she didn't miss much if she missed school dinners. It was spinach pie again today!

E Well, that's not the point, is it, Gilbert? He just didn't oughta have gone and done such a mean thing. I tell you, Gilbert, I've done gone and told the headteacher all about it!

G (Worried) You have? Your friend wouldn't happen to be . . . Florrie Fraggle, would it?

E Why it sure is!

G And you told the headteacher all about it, you say?

E I sure did. Mind you, my friend, Florrie, being such a nice person an' all, why, she wouldn't even tell me who this mean guy is. Says she don't want to make him look bad in front of the whole school an' all. I tell you, Gilbert, whoever that mean old person is, he just don't deserve a friend like Florrie.

G *(Feeling guilty)* Er . . . guess not.

E Well, I'm off to find Florrie and see if she's feelin' any better. See ya!

G Bye.

Exit Emeline.

Voice of Heart (or Conscience), offstage

H Cough! Cough!

G Who are you?

H I'm your heart, actually.

G My heart? *(Looks at chest)* What are you doing out here?

H Well, I've come out to make a complaint.

G A complaint? What do you mean?

H You're making me feel really bad with all the nasty things you keep doing. You're killing me, you know.

G Killing you?

H Yes, you're filling me up with badness. I need a clean-up operation in here.

G What do you mean? How can I clean you up?

H You need to get rid of all that badness. Only one way to do that too . . . through Jesus.

G Jesus?

H Yes. Only Jesus can make you clean from wrong things. You need to ask him to forgive you – that is, if you're sorry, of course – and he will. Then you need to see Florrie and say 'sorry' to her too for being so unkind. Ask her to forgive you too.

G Now, let me get this right. If I'm sorry, I ask Jesus to forgive me, and then do the same to Florrie. Right?

H Right!

G *(After thought)* Well, I am sorry actually, because I shouldn't have done it – and especially when she was so nice and didn't tell who it was. Yes, Lord Jesus, I am definitely sorry and I won't do it again.

H Good. Well go and sort it out with Florrie then.

G What, now?

H Straightaway. No good waiting around. Go on, go for it!

Exit Heart.

G Right . . . Florrie! *(Calls and moves offstage)*

NB: There needs to be some explanation of what we mean when we say the 'heart' or children may possibly think of our physical heart! If preferred, the Heart or Conscience need not be mentioned but the sketch could end by Gilbert reflecting some thoughts about how kind Florrie was not to tell, how she was always kind to him and that he was wrong to steal her sweets and dinner money. He could then decide to go and say 'sorry'.

I CAN'T GET IN

Teaching point

- enter his gates with thanksgiving and his courts with praise

Characters

Adult and Emeline (any puppet will do)

Enter Emeline at back of room, shouting.

E Heather! *(Adult's name)* . . . I can't get in!

A You can't get in?

E No, I can't get through the gate!

A Whatever do you mean, you can't get through the gate?

E *(Frustrated)* Oh! I just can't get in!

A Oh, I think I know why. You need to come in saying 'Thank you'.

E Thank you? You mean like a password?

A Well, sort of.

E Oh, right. Thank you . . . Thank you . . . THANK YOU! . . . It's not working!

A No, not like that, Emeline. Think of all the things you can thank God for and then try again.

E Oh, right. *(Thinks)* Thank you, God, for . . . Florrie's party . . . Thank you, God, for . . . McDonald's. *('Thank you' prayers gather momentum as Emeline takes steps forward towards adult)* Thank you, God, for my friends . . . and that we had great fun yesterday. Thank you, God, for my mum and dad and for Jesus and . . . *(Emeline now half-way towards adult)*

A That's right, Emeline. Well done.

E Hey! I'm in!

A Well, not quite. If you want to come right in the word is 'Praise'.

E Praise?

A That's right. Now begin to really praise God.

E Oh, right! . . . *(Thinks)* Praise you, Lord, you're great! *(Emeline walks right up to the adult as she speaks)* You're powerful and . . . loving and . . . kind. You give me everything I need. You're just wonderful and . . .

A That's it! You've done it!

E Wow! I'm in! *(Emeline turns round, surprised to see the audience)* . . . Hey! Look at all these people! Have they all come in praising and thanking God?

A Well, we'll see shall we?

Leader may then read Psalm 100 from 'The Message' Bible, which says:

'On your feet now – applaud Yahweh! Bring a gift of laughter, sing yourselves into his presence. Know this: Yahweh is God and God, Yahweh. He made us; we didn't make him. We're his people, his well-tended sheep. Enter with the password: "Thank you!" Make yourselves at home, talking praise. Thank him. Worship him. For Yahweh is sheer beauty, all-generous in love, loyal always and ever.'

IN A WHILE

Teaching points
- the consequences of disobedience
- not putting things off!

Characters
Ernie and Mum

Props
tape recording of sound effects:
1. Dad falling over roller skates, yelling 'Ernie'
2. Crunching sounds as car backs over Ernie's bike

dirty shorts, broken piece of bike

Enter Mum, talking to Ernie.

M Ernie, did you move your roller skates from the top of the stairs?

E Not yet, Mum, I'll do it in a while.

M No. Go and do it now, please, before someone falls over them.

E But Mum . . .

M No 'buts', please, Ernie. Do it now!

(Sound effect no. 1)

E *(Giggles)*

M It's not funny, Ernie. Come on, it's time you were getting ready for school.

Exit Ernie to look for his PE kit. Mum ad lib to audience about how untidy Ernie is, etc.
Re-enter Ernie.

E *(Shouts)* Mum? Where are my football shorts?

M I don't know.

E Have they been washed?

M Were they in the washing basket?

E *(Hesitating)* I'm not sure.

M Well, where did you put them when I told you to put them in the washing?

E Er . . . on the floor, I think . . . in the corner!

M Well that's where they'll be, then.

Mum moves across and picks up dirty shorts.

E Oh, Mum, they're filthy and I need them today. Old Bannister'll kill me when he sees these.

M Tough, Ernie. You should have thought of that when you chose not to do as you were told.

E But, Mum . . . I was going to do it . . . in a while!

M Oh, by the way, Ernie, did you move your bike away from the garage doors?

E No, not yet, Mum. I'll do it in a while!

M Well, Dad will want to get his car out in a minute and your bike will be in the way.

(Sound effect no. 2)

M & E Oh no!

Mum rushes to side stage and comes back with a broken piece of bike.

E *(Shocked)* Ohh Mum!! I was going to move it in a while.

M Too late, son. You chose to ignore me when I asked you to move it and now it will cost you a lot. And you'll have to walk to school too.

E But Mum . . .

M And do you know something else, Ernie?

E *(Sulkily)* What?

M It will take you quite a while!

Exit Mum and Ernie.

JUST RIGHT FOR YOU

Teaching point

- God gave us a present that was just right for us – Jesus. *(Possible Christmas theme)*

Characters

Florrie and Gilbert

Enter puppets, talking about Christmas.

F Hi, Gilbert. Eh, I'm so excited. It's nearly Christmas. I just can't wait to open my presents.

G Yeah! It's going to be great!

F Hey, Gilbert, what do you want for Christmas?

G *(Thinks)* Er . . . well . . . I know. I'd like lots and lots of sweets. Loads of sweets. Enough for every day until next Christmas!

F Oh Gilbert, that would be far too many. You'd get bad teeth and you'd feel really sick if you ate that many sweets.

G No I wouldn't.

F Yes you would.

G Wouldn't.

F Well I think you would – but anyway what else would you like?

G Umm . . . yes, I know . . . I'd like a motor bike. Yeah! Think about it . . .

F But you're too young for a motor bike.

G No! You can get them small enough for people like me now. And you can ride them as long as you don't go on the roads. Hey! I could go scrambling round the fields behind the school. I could go really fast and make lots of mud fly everywhere.

F Sounds as if that could be very dangerous to me. I don't think that's a very good present for you at all. Isn't there something else you'd like?

G Er . . . well I'd like some boxing gloves.

F Boxing gloves?

G Yeah, if I had some boxing gloves, I could bash people up. I could get boxing lessons and knock people out if I didn't like them or they annoyed me.

F Well that's stupid! You could get yourself into lots of trouble going round bashing people up. And you might get hurt yourself!

G Not if I get them first!

F Oh, come on, Gilbert, there must be something that you want that is sensible.

G Well, I would quite like one of the latest computers. I could play games on it.

F Well, that would be great, but computers cost a lot of money and I don't think your mum and dad will be able to afford that. Do you?

G Umm. Perhaps not. Well, what do you want for Christmas anyway, Florrie?

F Now I'd really like a new dress. One that I could go to parties in – one that was all sparkly and . . .

G Ugh! *(Mimics)* 'Do you like my new dress? – my pretty, pretty new dress!'

F Don't be so unkind, Gilbert.

G Well, what else would you like?

F I'd like . . . Hippity!

G Hippity? What's that?

F It's a Beanie Buddy. He's a lovely, big, green rabbit. He's all soft and fluffy and cuddly and . . .

G They're babyish, they are.

F No they're not. Lots of grown-ups collect them too!

G Anyway, you've got loads of Beanie Babies already. Isn't there anything else you want?

F Well, I'd really like a new bike.

G That's going to be a lot of money as well.

F Maybe it is, but anyway, I don't mind because I know that whatever I get, it won't be dangerous or get me into trouble. It will be just right for me.

G How do you know?

F Because my mum and dad will only give me what's good for me and what they know I will like.

G Oh!

F And I expect your mum and dad are the same, Gilbert, and you will get what is just right for you.

G I wonder what that will be?

F I wonder.

Exit Gilbert and Florrie still talking about presents.

LIFE TO THE FULL

Teaching point
- God wants us to experience life to the full

Characters
Adult and Caterpillar puppet and a pair of attachable wings

Enter Adult and Caterpillar.

A Good morning, little Caterpillar.

C Good? What's good about it? That's what I want to know.

A It's a lovely day. Look, the sun is shining . . .

C Huh! You might think the sun is good but it dries up my skin something terrible. I have to spend a fortune on wrinkle cream.

A Listen! The birds are singing . . .

C I can hear them all right. They keep me awake making that dreadful row. I need my beauty sleep, you know. You can't wonder I've got more lines on my face than a wrinkled prune.

A My word, you are in a bad mood. What's your name?

C *(Aggressively)* What's it got to do with you?

A I'm just trying to be friendly. Don't bite my head off!

C Well, if you really want to know, it's Kevin.

A Well, you've got a terrific garden here, Kevin. Have you lived here long?

C Too long! You're nosey, aren't yer?

A Well, I'm interested in you. What's wrong with living here, anyway?

C I'm fed up. I'm eating greens all day long – and I'll tell you summat else – I dice with death every time them birds are looking for something to eat. There's got to be more to life than this.

A But there is!

C Like what, for instance?

A Don't you know that God made you especially, and he wants to be friends with you.

C Oh no! Nobody made me. I grew from an egg. I know that 'cos me mum told me.

A Yes, that's true – but it's God who made you come alive in the first place. He really wants you to enjoy life.

C Enjoy life?

A Yes. Look around you and you can see all the things he's made. Look at all the colours – and take a sniff of these smells. And it's not all green you know. Don't you like a bit of juicy apple sometimes?

C Well . . . yes.

A God has lots of good plans for you too.

C Plans? I can't see no plans. How do I know it's true?

A It tells you in the Bible. It says if you really want to change . . .

C Oh, I could do with a change. I was going to go away for a fortnight to that Majorca *(Sound the J)*. That'll be a nice change.

A Not that sort of a change. I mean, if you really want to change so that you can see all the things there are to enjoy, and you want to get rid of all your grumpy old ways, then tell Jesus about it. Tell him you're really sorry for being so horrible and ask him to come and be your friend. You'll change, believe me, and you'll see that life will be wonderful.

C Do you really think so? It's worth a try, I suppose. I'll go and do it now. I'm beginning to feel so sleepy. *(Yawns)*

Exit Caterpillar and attaches wings. Adult ad lib to audience re caterpillar. Re-enters.

A Hello again, Caterpillar.

C Oh 'ello. Let's have a stretch. Mmm . . . oh, I say . . . it's a lovely day, isn't it?

A It certainly is.

C Feel that warm sun . . . and listen to those dear little birds.

A Yes, they do sound lovely, don't they? Er . . . you don't think they're a bit loud for you? . . . And the sun too bright perhaps?

C Good gracious no! Whatever made you say that?

A Just something you said before you went for your long sleep. Before you asked Jesus to be your friend.

C Well, I feel different now. *(Notices wings and shrieks)* . . . Get it off! Get it off!

A Get what off?

C On me back! Quick! There's something on me back. Get it off!

A: Hold on. Stop wriggling. Look, it's nothing to worry about. You've grown some wings. God has given you a pair of wings.

C What for?

A To fly with, of course.

C Fly? You mean up in the air? Oh no, I couldn't do that. I'm scared of heights.

A Don't be frightened – if God has given you wings, then he knows you can use them properly. All you have to do is stretch them out and take off. Go on. Have a go!

C All right. Hang on a minute. Here I go now. Wheeeeee! . . . I can fly! Oh, I say, everything looks really different from up here. You know that big blackbird that always plagued the life out of me – well he looks really tiny from up here. Hey, titch, look at me! You were right. Everything's wonderful now. Wheeeeee! . . . Thank you, Jesus!

Exit Adult and 'Caterpillar'.

MAKE THE RIGHT CHOICE

Teaching points
- making right choices
- choosing good leaders

Characters
Florrie and Ernie

Enter Ernie, thinking! Enter Florrie.

F Hey, Ernie. What are you doing?

E Just thinking!

F Be careful! You're not used to it.

E Oi, watch it!

F Well, what's going through that under-used brain of yours? *(Ernie looks puzzled)* What are you thinking about?

E People in my class.

F Oh? What for?

E Mr Hunter said that we were going to have one person to be like a team captain for our class. Someone who we thought would be our class leader. Well I was wondering who would be a good person.

F And who have you thought of?

E Oh, a few people . . .

F Like who?

E Freddie.

F Freddie?

E Yeah! He'd be really good. He'd make everyone do what he wanted. If they didn't, he'd bash 'em up! He's really strong. He goes to the gym and does body building.

F But he's a bully! Have you forgotten when he stole your lunch? He sat on you 'til you gave it to him. And who wants to do what *he* wants anyway?

E Mmm. Well, there's Mick. He's the best runner in the school and he's a brilliant footballer.

F So?

E What do you mean, 'So'?

F I mean what has that got to do with being a good class leader? Anyway, he's a show-off. *(Pause)* What about Ricky? *(Goes into a 'dream')*

E *(Laughs)* Ricky?

F Don't be horrible. Everyone thinks Ricky is really nice.

E You mean you sloppy girls think Ricky is 'really, really nice' *(Mimics)*.

Well he is!

E Just because he gels his hair and wears all the latest trendy gear! And he only thinks about himself and what he looks like. *(Makes fun of him)* 'Don't do that, you'll mess up my hair!'

F Stop it! You're horrible, you are! It's a good job you're not going to be our class captain!

E Hey! I never thought of that. Perhaps people will choose me!

F You must be joking!

E I think I'd be very good.

F Why? Go on. What makes you think you would make a good leader?

Pause while Ernie considers the question – unsuccessfully!

F There you are, you see! I bet you don't even know what a good class captain should be like, do you?

E Well, we've never had one before, have we?

F No, but Mr Hunter said it had to be someone who was fair and honest and who everyone would take notice of. And it might be someone who we wouldn't think of immediately.

E Like me, you mean?

F You'd be the *last* person anyone would think of!

E No, I wouldn't.

F Would!

E Wouldn't! The last person anyone would think of would be someone like . . . Billy, not me!

F Billy!!

E Eh?

F Ernie, that's it! Billy would make a brilliant class captain. *(Ernie looks puzzled)* Think about it! He's fair and honest. He doesn't show off or think he's great. He thinks about other people. Remember when Ranjit first came to school and he couldn't speak very much English and didn't know anyone. Who looked after him and made him feel welcome? Even Freddie stopped making fun of him when Billy told him to stop.

E But he's little and weedy and . . .

F To look at, yes, but that's not important, is it?

E No, I guess not. But you could have all that and good looks as well if you chose someone else.

F Like who?

Ernie shows off, touching up his hair.

E Well . . .

F You won't look good when I've finished with you.

Exit Ernie, chased by Florrie.

MAKING UP

Teaching point
• Jesus brings reconciliation

Characters
Gilbert, Ernie and Jasper

Props
football

Enter Gilbert and Ernie, quarrelling.

E Not friends with you.

G So what! Who cares?

E Not me!

G Not me either.

E *You* cheated!

G Didn't!

E Did!

G You don't know the rules.

E Who says?

G I do!

E Well, who do you think you are, anyway?

G I'm the captain.

E Only because you're old Jones' favourite.

G No it's not. It's because . . . well . . . I'm a better player than you.

E What a joke! Who's scored the most goals this season?

G Not you.

E Yes I have!

G Haven't!

E Have!

G Show off!

E Wouldn't play with you again if you paid me.

G Wouldn't play with you either . . . big ears!

E Big ape!

G Oh, I hate you!

E I hate you too!

Gilbert and Ernie move away from one another, turning their backs towards each other. Enter Jasper.

J *(To Ernie)* Hi, Ernie. Want a game of football?

E Yeah!

J OK. See you in the park in a few minutes.

E Right. Great!

Exit Ernie, stage right.

J *(To Gilbert)* Hey, Gilbert. Want a game of football?

G Yeah!

J See you in the park in a few minutes.

G OK. Great!

Exit Gilbert, stage left. Exit Jasper.
Re-enter Ernie and Gilbert from opposite sides.

E & G What are you doing here?

E & G I've come to play football with Jasper.

E & G I didn't know he was your friend!

Re-enter Jasper with football

J Are you ready?

E & G *(Hesitatingly)* Oh . . . OK!

Exit Jasper, Ernie and Gilbert

NEVERLASTING (PART 1)

Teaching point
- unfaithfulness

Characters
Adult, Ernie and Florrie

Enter Ernie, obviously waiting for someone. Enter Adult

A Hello, Ernie. What are you doing?

E Oh, I'm waiting for my friend.

A Oh, who's that?

E Er . . . just a friend.

A You've gone all red, Ernie! Who is this friend?

E *(Coyly)* Er . . . Myrtle.

A Myrtle? Oh, your friend is a *girl*!

E *(Looks a bit embarrassed)* She's my girlfriend.

A Oh, I see. No need to be embarrassed. Has she been your girlfriend very long?

E Ages and ages. She gives me sweets and lets me share her lunch. She said she's bought me a present – a Manchester United scarf. *(Change to relevant football club)* And she's invited me to her party on Saturday.

A That'll be nice.

E Yes. She says she loves me lots and lots and lots. She told me she'll love me for ever and ever, and never stop.

A That's great, Ernie. Perhaps you can introduce me to her sometime. Anyway I must be going now. I'll see you later.

Exit Adult. Enter Florrie.

F Ernie!

E Yeah?

F You know Myrtle?

E Of course I know Myrtle. She's my girlfriend.

F Well, she's just told me she isn't any more!

E What?

F She doesn't want to be friends with you.

E Never! I'm waiting for her now!

F Well, I don't think she'll be coming.

E Of course she will – she's just a bit late, that's all.

F She told me she's not asking you to her party on Saturday.

E You're making it up!

F No I'm not. You ask her. She says she doesn't love you any more.

E After all this time?

F And anyway – she's got a new boyfriend now.

E No she hasn't.

F Yes she has!

E Hasn't!

F Has!

E Who?

F Barney Fraggle! I've seen her sharing her lunch with him.

E Barney Fraggle? Never!

F Yeah! They were sitting in the park together, holding hands. And d'you know what he was wearing?

E What?

F A new *(Man United)* scarf

E Oh no!

Exit Florrie and Ernie (sadly).

NEVERLASTING (PART 2)

Teaching points
- disappointments
- God never changes

Characters
Billy Joe and Gilbert

Enter Billy Joe and Gilbert, talking.

G Cor! You are lucky!

BJ I know.

G When did you hear you were going to Disneyworld?

BJ Yesterday. My dad 'phoned up. He said he'd just bought a villa in Florida where we can go for our holidays.

G Bought it?

BJ Yeah! He's dead rich. I can have anything I want.

G Anything?

BJ Yeah, my dad works abroad where they get oil. He owns a big oil well and makes lots and lots of money.

G So you can have anything you want?

BJ Yeah, anything! I've got my own special motorbike. And our house in Spain has got a big swimming pool and we have servants to look after us. We've had it for ages. And when I go there, my dad owns a riding stable and I've got two horses.

G Wow! You must be rich. I bet your dad's really famous, too.

BJ Yeah, he is.

G Hey. Is your dad called Wightman?

BJ Yeah, why?

G Only there's a picture here . . .

BJ Let me see! *(Reads)* Oh, no!

G What's up?

BJ Dad's oil well has dried up. He's gone bankrupt!

G So? What does that mean?

BJ Well, it means he's lost all his money. He'll have to sell everything.

G Never!

BJ Yeah.

G Looks like you're not going to Disneyworld after all.

Exit Billy Joe and Gilbert.

SPREADING THE WORD

Teaching point
- God wants to use us in evangelism

Characters
Ernie and Florrie

Enter Ernie and Florrie.

F Hey, Ernie!

E Yes, Florrie?

F God wants to use you.

E Use me?

F Yes.

E Are you sure it's me he wants to use?

F Yes, I told you already.

E How?

F He wants you to help him make his kingdom grow.

E I don't know what you mean.

F He wants you to tell people about Jesus so they can believe in him and go to heaven.

E Is that where God's kingdom is then – heaven?

F Well, yes and no! God's kingdom is everywhere that he rules. Everywhere that he's King. Everywhere that he's boss!

E Well, Jesus is our King . . . So, let me get this right. Do you mean that everywhere God's people are, that's where his kingdom is?

F Exactly!

E But this is a very big job and I'm much too small to do it.

F No you're not, Ernie. It doesn't matter how small you are, God can still use you.

E But I don't know enough.

F You know that God loves you, don't you?

E Of course I do.

F And you know that all the wrong things we do spoil our friendship with God, don't you?

E Yes.

F And you know that Jesus came and died to take our sin away?

E Yes. You know I do!

F And you know that by believing in Jesus and saying sorry for all the wrong things we have done God will forgive us, don't you?

E *(A little impatient)* Yes.

F Then you know enough. All you've got to do is start telling people so that they can be in God's kingdom too.

E But where do I start?

F Start by telling just one person.

E But what if they won't listen?

F Don't worry about that. It's like planting a seed. All you have to do is plant God's word in someone's heart and leave God to make it grow into something.

E But just one person isn't going to make much difference, is it? That's hardly going to make God's kingdom grow.

F But that one will go and tell someone else, and then there'll be . . .?

E Two.

F And those two will tell someone else and then there'll be . . .?

E Four.

F That's right. And then those four will tell four more and then there'll be . . .?

E Um . . . *(Tries to count fingers)* . . . Seven.

F Oh, Ernie, your sums are dreadful! *(Asks audience)* . . . Eight – that's it. And if those eight tell eight more that will be . . .?

E Eighty-eight!!

F Oh really, Ernie. *(Asks audience)* That's right – sixteen.

E Oh! Still, I do get the picture. If everyone tells someone else, God's kingdom will grow very quickly, won't it? And all from little old me starting it off!

F Yes . . . amazing isn't it?

E It sure is. *(Exits shouting)* Hey, Eric! I want to tell you something.

Exit Ernie and Florrie, discussing who they will tell first.

THE GARAGE SALE

Teaching points
- the parable of the treasure and the pearl
- giving all for God

Characters
Billy Joe and Florrie

Props
a notice saying 'Garage Sale Here Today'

Enter Florrie and Billy Joe, talking about the notice.

F Are your mum or dad having a garage sale, then?

BJ No! I am!

F You?

BJ Yes!

F What for?

BJ Because there's something very expensive that I want to buy.

F What?

BJ Well, you know I collect Beanie Babies? Well there's one very rare one called (Humphrey) that I really want and there's one for sale on the internet, and I'm going to buy it.

F Oh! So what are you selling at this garage sale?

BJ Well, my roller blades.

F What! You're selling your roller blades?

BJ Yes!

F But you're always playing on them, and they are quite new. Why are you selling them? Don't you like roller blading any more?

BJ Yes, but this Beanie Baby is really expensive, and Mum and Dad say if I really want it then I have to get the money. And my roller blades will get me lots of money.

F Wow! What else are you selling?

BJ My skateboard, football, some computer games – well, all my computer games . . .

F But you saved up for ages to buy those.

BJ I know, but I'd rather have this Beanie Baby.

F I think you're mad!

BJ I don't care. I know that I really want this Beanie Baby, and I'm going to get it if I have to sell everything I've got.

F So, is this Beanie Baby worth a lot of money then?

BJ Hundreds of dollars!

F But you are not going to get enough from just one garage sale.

BJ Probably not! But I've already got quite a lot.

F How did you get that?

BJ I sold my collection of Beanie Babies.

F What? But I thought you wanted this one to add to your collection?

BJ This one is worth more than all the others put together.

F I can't believe it! You've sold your Beanie Babies? All of them?

BJ Yes! . . . Don't look so surprised. You'd do the same if you wanted something badly enough.

F I don't think I would. . . . So what if people don't want to buy what you are selling in this garage sale?

BJ Oh, they will, everybody wants a bargain, don't they?

F Mm! . . . How much are you selling your roller blades for?

BJ Are you interested in buying them?

F I might be.

BJ Depends how much people offer me for them.

F What do you mean?

BJ Well, this garage sale is an auction. People have to say what they will pay for each item, and the item is sold to the person who will pay the most.

F So, they might not get a bargain?

BJ Depends on how much they think something is worth, and what they are willing to pay. So, how much are you willing to pay for my roller blades then? They are quite new and have only been used by one careful owner – me!

F But someone might say they will pay more than me.

BJ Right! So you will have to decide how badly you want them – like I had to do with my new Beanie Baby!

F Mmm . . . I'll have to think about that. . . . What time does the garage sale start?

BJ 3 o'clock.

F I might just have time to go and get some money out of my savings . . . now how much have I got in there? . . . let me think . . .

Exit Florrie and Billy Joe.

THE NEWS

Teaching points
- giving
- helping those in need

Characters
Gilbert, Newscaster

Props
Box made to look like a television with a paper screen on which is drawn the face of a newscaster. (Alternatively you can use a real television which needs to be facing away from the audience). A banana, sweets, bag of crisps, can of drink, 'Neighbours' music.

Newscaster hidden behind model television!
Gilbert sitting watching the news. He is stuffing himself with bananas, crisps, sweets, drinks, etc.

N And now for today's news. Famine is spreading over Africa as thousands starve to death. African governments have made an urgent plea to the rest of the world to send aid . . . to send aid . . . to send aid . . . to send aid . . .

G Oh no! Telly's on the blink again.

Gilbert goes over to thump it. As he does so, the newscaster's hand comes through the paper screen and grabs him. (Alternatively, if using a real television, make sure the puppet is facing the audience and the television is facing the puppet. Then the words of the newscaster can come from offstage.)

N Oi, you!

G Eh, watch it! Let me go. What do you think you're doing?

N *(Releases Gilbert)* I'm trying to get your attention, actually.

G What do you mean? I've been watching you ever since you came on.

N Ah, you might have been watching, but you've not really been listening.

G I have!

N Go on then. Tell me what I just said.

G You said . . . Um! . . . Er! . . .

N There you are you see. I knew you didn't know. You had that glazed look in your eye!

G I do know too! You said something about Africa – millions starving to death. See!

N Exactly!

G Exactly what?

N And you sit there stuffing your face with all that food.

G Yes . . . well? So what!

N Haven't you ever thought about it? There you sit with . . . what have you got exactly?

G Crisps, chocolates, a can of coke, sandwiches, a banana, a sausage . . .

N Haven't you ever stopped to think that it's not fair?

G No.

N Well it's not, is it? You've got all this and they've got nothing.

G Well that's not my fault, is it? There's nothing I can do about it.

N Of course there is.

G What? I can hardly post them my sausage, can I? And my chocolates would melt in all that heat, wouldn't they?

N Ha, ha, very funny. I'll tell you what you could do, though.

G What's that?

N Don't buy any sweets and things for two days each week and the money you save you could send to one of the charities who send aid.

G Well that won't do much, will it?

N Nonsense! You could feed someone for a whole day for about 50 pence in Africa.

G 50p? Is that all?

N Yep. Not much, is it? Especially when you've got so much.

G Well, I suppose not.

N You'll give it a go then?

G OK. You've talked me into it! I will.

N Well done! You'll feel so much better if you do.

G Thanks for pointing it out, mate.

N Not at all. And now I think normal service can be resumed, don't you? 'And now for the weather. Things are looking so much better now. There should be a much brighter start to tomorrow – dark clouds are beginning to lift, especially over Africa. And now coming up next – something we all need.'

(Music of 'Neighbours')

Exit Gilbert and Newscaster

THE PUPPET RACE

Teaching points

- laying down our life for a friend
- Jesus died to save us

Characters

Commentator, Starter and 4 puppets, Ernie, Gilbert, Jasper and Charlie.

Props

Taped sound of crowd noise throughout, swelling at appropriate times, etc.

Low crowd noise which increases and decreases as is appropriate. Enter Starter and 4 puppets warming up on the starting line.

C *(In the style of a racing commentator)* And now the crowd roars as the four contestants for the final of the men's 400 metres begin warming up on the starting line. The atmosphere is electric in the auditorium this afternoon. Who will take the prize home with them today? These runners have been training all year for this event. There's not much to choose between them.

Will it be Charlie? *(Charlie steps forward, showing himself to the crowd as the crowd noise swells, etc.)* Otherwise known as 'The Charger', solid and dependable. He's a fighter, a very powerful runner.

Or what about Ernie? *(Ernie steps forward, taking a bow)* Last year's winner, the present holder of the cup. Still a very good runner, light on his feet, known as 'Speedy'. He's still in very good form by the look of him.

(Gilbert steps forward, running rapidly on the spot) Oh and just look at 'Galloping Gilbert'! Look at him go! Well I must say he looks in very good shape too, although he has been known to break a few rules in the past – not the most popular here today. Got himself disqualified last year for barging, but nevertheless it certainly looks as though he's in with a good chance today!

(Jasper steps forward, showing off his long legs!) And yes, it's 'The Giant'. Jasper, better known as 'The Giant' because of his long legs. Another powerful runner. Could it be his turn to win the race today? And now they're under starter's orders . . .

S On your marks, get set, GO! *(Fires cap-gun?)*

Exit Starter.
Puppets on an imaginary line, run on the spot continually, taking steps forward as indicated.

C And they're off. All of them off to a good start . . . but it's Charlie just in the lead *(Charlie takes one step forward)* . . . now quickly followed by Galloping Gilbert *(Gilbert takes one step forward)* . . . So it's Gilbert and Charlie in the lead . . . but wait . . . here comes Jasper and his giant strides take him into the lead. *(Jasper takes two steps forward)* And now here comes Ernie, fast as lightning, chasing down the track, going into the lead just ahead of Jasper. *(Ernie takes three steps forward)* But Gilbert and Charlie won't be beaten *(Gilbert and Charlie both take one step forward)* . . . and it's neck and neck! If anything, Gilbert is moving slightly ahead. *(Gilbert takes one step forward)* Well! What a surprise! The excitement is rising in the auditorium. It's anybody's race. Oh and here come the others making a challenge. *(Jasper and Charlie take one step, Ernie takes two steps forward)* But it's Ernie! . . . It's Ernie in the lead now . . . He's forging ahead! *(Ernie takes another step forward)* Could this be victory for Ernie? The crowd are urging him on, he's a very popular contestant and the favourite to win this race here today. I must say the others are beginning to look a bit tired already . . . but no sign of Ernie tiring, in fact he's increasing his lead! *(Ernie takes another step forward)*

C But what's this? Gilbert is staging a comeback . . . he's galloping down the track now. *(Gilbert takes two steps forward and falls over!)* Oh dear! He's down. Galloping Gilbert is down! Listen to the crowd roar . . . what a terrible shame! He's out of the race. The other runners are still going for it. *(Jasper, Ernie and Charlie all take one step forward)* The crowd are urging Gilbert to get up and carry on: 'Come on, Gilbert, you can do it!'

But no, Gilbert seems to have really hurt himself. Jasper and Charlie are looking across at Gilbert . . . they certainly don't look too concerned about it.

But wait a minute! Ernie is looking back now. *(Ernie turns round to see Gilbert)* That will slow him down . . . surely he's not thinking of going back to help Gilbert. He'll lose the race if he does. He seems to be hesitating and meanwhile here come Jasper and Charlie *(Jasper and Charlie both take one step forward)* But it's still Ernie in the lead. Gilbert's getting up but he looks in a bad way . . . he's trying to run . . . He wants to finish the race. *(Gilbert staggers up and limps on the spot.)*

But look! Ernie is looking back again at Gilbert. *(Ernie glances back)* The crowd is roaring for Ernie to finish the race and win as Jasper and Charlie are neck and neck and closing the gap. *(Jasper and Charlie both take 1 step forward)* And yes! Would you believe it? Ernie is going back. He's going back to help Gilbert to the finishing line. *(Ernie goes back to Gilbert)* He's throwing away his chances of winning. This will certainly put him right out of the race. The crowd are shocked, they don't know what to make of it all. So it's between Jasper and Charlie now as they fight it out for first and second place. *(Jasper and Charlie both take two steps forward)*

But here comes Jasper with a new burst of energy *(Jasper takes one step forward)* . . . and Charlie doesn't seem to have anything left *(Charlie slows)* as Jasper increases his lead. *(Jasper takes one step forward)* And yes, it's going to be Jasper 'The Giant' first over the line *(Jasper crosses finishing line)* followed by a very tired Charlie. But the race isn't over yet, folks! Here come the losers, Ernie and Gilbert, limping home. And listen to the crowd cheering them in. They're standing and clapping and shouting for Ernie. He may not have won the race, but he has certainly won the crowd.

Exit Commentator and puppets.

THE VIP

Teaching point
- everyone is important and has a job to do for God

Characters
Gilbert, Worm

Props
apple

Enter Gilbert, standing eating an apple. Worm enters and looks at him.

G What d'yer think you're looking at?

W Nothing.

G Well clear off then – I hate stupid worms!

W I'm not stupid.

G Well you look stupid to me. All worms are useless.

W I'll have you know I'm not useless! I'm a very important person!

G *(Sarcastically)* Oh well, I do beg your pardon, only I never knew we had a VIP coming today! *(In exaggerated posh accent)* H'I'd have put the red carpet out if H'I'd known, Your Majesty!

W Well, if you're going to be sarcastic, then . . .

G Well, what makes you think you're so important anyway? *I'm* more important than you!

W No, you're not.

G Yes I am.

W Not!

G Am!

W What can you do that's good then?

G Well . . . I can swing from that big tree there to that one over there.

W So?

G Well, you can't, can you?

W Nope!

G And I bet you can't eat twelve bananas at one go, can you?

W No – but then I haven't got such a big mouth as you, have I?

G Oi, watch it, worm!

W Anyway, that doesn't prove a thing. I'm still more important than you.

G Oh yes? What can you do then?

W Dig tunnels in the ground.

G Big deal! That's not exactly earth-shattering, is it?

W It is, actually. If I didn't do what I do you'd go hungry.

G How do you work that one out?

W 'Cos when I dig tunnels, the air gets into the ground – it breaks up and then things grow better. That banana tree, for example – you wouldn't have any bananas to eat if I didn't do my bit under the ground. In fact the whole world might starve!

G You're a nut case you are. Go away!

W Shan't!

G If you don't clear off I'll tread on you and squash you flat!

W Anyway, my cousin's gonna get you.

G Oh, big deal!

W He will. He'll make you holler, I can tell you.

G *(Sarcastically)* Oh, I'm very frightened of your skinny little cousin. Look, I'm shaking!

W Well, my cousin will make you sorry.

G So where is this Arnold Schwarzenegger cousin of yours then that's gonna get me? *(Takes a bite of the apple)*

W Well, he was in that apple. You've just eaten him and you're gonna feel really bad soon!

G Gulp!

Exit Gilbert and Worm.

TOP OF THE LIST

Teaching point
- putting God first

Characters
Ernie and Florrie

Enter Ernie and Florrie.

F So what's top of your list then, Ernie?

E What? Oh, don't bother me now . . .

F You know, the list from Mrs Davies at school.

E Look, I'm busy playing . . . it's a silly list anyway.

F No, it's not! You've got to name the three things which are most important to you.

E Easy! Food, food and food! Now go away.

F Oh come on, Ernie. You've got to think more than that.

E OK. McDonald's, fish and chips and . . . cheesy wotsits!

F No, Ernie. Really! The three most important things.

E Er . . . I am quite fond of my toe-nail collection. Oh, I don't know. Give me some clues.

F Well, Mr McCoy would put his car at the top of his list. He's always out washing it and polishing it.

E Yeah! And what about Charlie? He's always on his computer. He never has time for anyone else. Sonic is definitely top of his list.

F So, now, what's the top of your list? What's most important to you?

E Oh, I don't know. What's your top three anyway?

F My top three?

E Yeah! Go on!

F Well . . . it's private.

E You wanted to know mine.

F OK, OK. Well, in third place it's my new bike. It's yellow with pink flowers on it.

E Ugh!

F What do you mean, 'Ugh'? It's lovely! And it's my first bike without stabilisers.

E OK. What's second?

F Hmm. I suppose it would be Mum and Dad.

E Mum and Dad! You're not serious! Mums and dads nag all the time.

F Yes, but they do love me and make sure I'm safe and not hungry.

E Oh, I suppose so. Well, what's top of your list then?

F Well . . . it's . . .

E Go on. Tell me.

F You'll laugh.

E No I won't. Come on.

F Promise?

E Promise.

F Well . . . it's . . .

E *(Interrupts)* I bet it's your funny doll. The one that's cries and wets itself. Yuk! Fancy a doll doing that! Disgusting!

F No, it's not. Don't be silly, Ernie.

E Or I bet it's your hamster, Hammy – the one that bit my finger last week.

F No, it's not that. Promise you won't laugh?

E OK. I promise.

F Well. It's God!

E God?

F Yes! God!

E Why? Aren't I more important to you than God? 'Cos I play with you . . . and share my sweets with you . . . sometimes!

F You are important to me, Ernie, and you are in my top ten, but God is first because . . . well, lots of things really.

E Tell me!

F He created the world. He's always there when I want to talk to him. He loves me and really, really cares about me – and about you!

E Oh, I guess I can see why he's top then.

F So, what's top of your list then, Ernie?

E My list?

F Yes, your list!

E Well, I . . . I . . . I . . . I . . .

F I knew it! YOU'RE top of your list! Oh, come on. Let's go and get our bikes out!

Exit Ernie and Florrie.

YOU'VE LOST YOUR PATIENCE

Teaching point
• need for patience *(Possible New Year's theme)*

Characters
Ernie and Florrie

Enter Ernie who talks to the audience about his resolution to become more patient.
Enter Flossie who talks slowly with a whiney voice!

F Hello, Ernie.

E *(Cheerfully)* Hi, Flossie.

F Well . . . you sound cheerful today, Ernie.

E I am.

F Oh? What's happened then?

E Well, I've decided to be more patient.

F *(Surprised)* You have?

E Yes! You remember how Mum is always telling me off about getting angry and losing my patience – well I'm going to do something about it.

F You are?

E That's right!

F Oh good! Perhaps you won't get so annoyed with me then. You're always losing your patience with me.

E No I'm not!

F Yes you are!

E *(Becoming impatient – stops himself)* Well . . . I know . . . and I'm sorry! But things are going to be different from now on.

F Oh great! *(Pause)* Hey, Ernie?

E *(Placidly)* Yes?

F *(Very whiney!)* You know what?

E What?

F You know your bedroom?

E *(Hesitatingly)* Yes . . .

F You know your (Lego) model?

E *(Simmering)* Yes . . .

F Well, I had to get something from your bedroom . . .

E *(Trying not to be impatient)* Yes . . .

F Well, you know what? *(Worriedly)* I'm afraid I knocked it over by mistake and . . .

E *(Annoyed)* You did what? *(Takes a deep breath)*

F I'm sorry, Ernie.

E *(Regains composure)* Well . . . never mind – I'm sure I can rebuild it. Let's forget about it, shall we? By the way, have you remembered that we are going to Billy Joe's and Emeline's this morning?

F Oh no! I forgot. I'll have to go and get ready.

E OK, but don't be long. We've only got five minutes.

F All right. Be back in a minute.

Exit Flossie.

Ernie talks to the audience about how good he's been not losing his patience with Flossie. He admits that he nearly lost it! Decides that he will count up to ten if he starts to feel impatient. Looks at watch. Comments about how long it takes girls to get ready.

E *(Shouts)* Are you ready yet?

F *(Calls from offstage)* Won't be a minute.

Ernie walks around getting more and more impatient! Starts to count. Reminds himself to keep calm.

E Come on, Flossie.

F Coming *(Enter Flossie)* . . . sorry I've been so long, Ernie.

E *(Snaps)* I should think so . . . too . . . *(Starts to count under breath)*

F Oh, Ernie?

E *(Patiently agitated)* Yes?

F You know what?

E *(Impatience mounting)* What?

F You know Billy Joe?

E *(Calms himself)* Yes . . .

F Well, you know what? You know your football?

E Yes!

F Well, you know you lost your football?

E *(Losing patience)* Yes . . .

F Well, you know what?

E *(Sharply)* What?

F I saw Billy Joe playing with it yesterday – at the park!

E *(Loses patience)* You did what?

Short pause.

F Ernie?

E *(Angrily)* What?

F You know what?

E WHAT?

F *(Whiney)* You've lost your patience!

Exit Ernie and Florrie.